The
CRAFTY HAND
Collection

CREATIVE
CANDLES

Chantal Truber
Photographs by Dominique Farantos

Aurum Press

INTRODUCTION

Making your own candles is one of the simplest ways of adding a personal touch to a dinner table or of bringing unusual and striking shapes and colours into your home.

Although they have such a long history, being man's first, and for a long time, only means of artificial light, it is only comparatively recently with the industrialized production of petroleum that candles could be easily and cheaply produced. Now, almost every craft shop stocks a range of moulds, and the simple raw materials – paraffin wax, stearin and wicks – that, with a few dyes, are all that is needed to make candles at home.

In the pages that follow, the basic techniques and materials you will need to make every possible type of candle are clearly explained. You will find that you already have much of the equipment required. Although many candles can be made from purpose-made moulds, which are widely available in craft shops, one of the pleasing aspects of candle-making is that almost any container can be pressed into service. As long as it can withstand the temperature of the hot wax and will not leak and as long as the candle can be easily turned out once it is set, you can use almost any vessel you wish. You can even add fragrances to your candles and, if you want to use them in your garden on a warm summer's evening, you can add a little anti-midge liquid to make them the perfect lighting for a barbecue.

The candles illustrated here are intended to inspire and encourage you to try out your own ideas. The stages involved in making each one are clearly explained, but you can change the shape, colour and size of every design as you wish. Few crafts offer so much scope for making unusual and attractive objects easily and inexpensively. And of course, if your first efforts do not work, simply melt them down and start again. Experiment and, above all, enjoy your new skills.

MATERIALS AND EQUIPMENT

WAXES

For convenience we have used the single word 'wax' for the materials that are melted down to make the candles described on the pages that follow. In fact, as you will see, different kinds of wax, both natural and man-made, can be used to achieve a range of effects, and you can also combine standard candlemaking wax with additives to colour, scent, texture or impart a gloss to the basic candle.

Beeswax

This is the king of materials for candlemaking. Until stearin was developed in the early nineteenth century, most people used candles made from tallow, a rendering of animal fats that smoked and smelt unpleasant. Because of the cost, only the wealthy and the church could afford candles made from beeswax.

Beeswax is sold in the form of beads or discs. Five per cent added to basic candlemaking wax will improve the appearance of the finished candle and help it to burn brightly and steadily. It is also available in pre-formed honeycomb sheets, which can be rolled to make candles.

Beeswax is expensive, but it is attractive to look at and to touch. In addition, it gives off the most wonderful aroma and burns with a steady, bright flame, giving off little smoke. It melts at about 62°C (144°F). Natural, or virgin, beeswax is a yellowish colour. You can also buy refined beeswax, which is white. As it ages, the white wax tends to turn yellow, but it can be treated with chemicals if you want to restore the original colour.

Natural or coloured wax sheets, smooth or honeycombed, both of which measure about 40 x 20cm (16 x 8in), are available from specialist suppliers (see Stockists, page 48). Wax beads and pellets are available from the same sources or from good craft shops.

Paraffin Wax

Paraffin waxes are a by-product of the oil-refining process, produced mostly by the distillation of petroleum. There is a range of grades, but all are white, odourless and tasteless.

Paraffin wax is widely available, in pellets or beads or in blocks of various shapes and sizes. It is sold either in pure form or mixed with stearin (see below).

Paraffin wax is solid at normal room temperature, and its melting point ranges between 40°C and 71°C (104–160°F), depending on how it was produced.

Paraffin wax is one of the two essential ingredients of basic candle wax. The other is stearin.

Stearin

This white, crystalline substance, which occurs naturally in many animal and vegetable fats, is used in the manufacture of soaps and adhesives, as well as in candles. Like paraffin wax, stearin is available in several forms – as a powder, in granules and in blocks of various shapes – and it is sold in the same kinds of outlet.

About 10 to 20 per cent of stearin is added to paraffin wax that is to be used for candles. It helps the wax to harden and makes it more opaque. Because it increases the degree of shrinkage, it also acts as a release agent, making it easier to free the finished candle from the mould (but see **Moulds**, page 8). Stearin also serves as a solvent for dyes (in fact, most candle dyes are little blocks of coloured stearin), and its inclusion intensifies the brightness of a colour. In addition, because stearin raises the melting point of paraffin wax, it helps to produce a longer burning candle that is less likely to bend or sag and that gives off little or no smoke.

It is possible to buy paraffin wax ready-mixed with stearin, so you do not have to worry about mixing the materials in the correct proportions.

Unless otherwise stated, all of the candles in this book were made with a mixture of paraffin wax and about 10 to 20 per cent stearin.

Powdered wax

This is a combination of equal parts of stearin and paraffin and a small amount of beeswax (or occasionally another kind of wax). It is sold in 1kg (2lb) bags, and although it is rather more expensive to buy it ready-mixed than to buy the ingredients separately, it gives an excellent finish to plain, smooth candles. In addition, candles made with powdered wax produce less smoke as they burn.

Powdered wax is easy to use. Choose your mould. Measure the volume, then use one and a half times that volume of powder for each candle. This kind of wax has a melting point of about 80°C (176°F), but see also page 36, where it is used in a slightly different way.

Mouldable Wax

This kind of wax does not need to be heated, which makes it ideal for children. It is easy to cut and shape and can be moulded simply by the warmth of your hands. It comes in slabs (about the size of a bar of chocolate) or small squares, in a range of about six colours. The different colours can be mixed together to produce new shades. The wax can be used on its own to make a candle or it can be used to decorate other waxes.

This kind of wax does tend to be quite fragile, so you must handle the finished candles carefully and wrap them in plenty of tissue paper or bubble-wrap if you are sending them as a gift.

Recycled Wax

It is possible to salvage wax from old candles, from experiments that have gone wrong and from candles that have broken. You can also reuse any wax left over from another project. Place all the bits in a double saucepan or bain-marie and add a colour that is darker than the resulting mix. If the finished candle looks rather dull, dip it into a bath of melted stearin, which will set to give a beautifully glossy coat.

OTHER MATERIALS

Colorants

Although there are occasions when you will want to keep the natural colour of wax, one of the great attractions of making your own candles is the enormous range of rich and subtle colours that you can create. You can use any colouring agent that will dissolve in the candle wax, including oil pastels, wax crayons, special wax dyes (which are available in discs, chips, powders, tubes) and colours that are sold for use with oil paint. There is also a wax whitener, which can be used with other colours when you want paler, more pastel tones. Remember, though, that whatever colouring agent you use must be soluble in candle wax.

If you use a disc wax dye, grate it and dissolve it in the stearin before adding it to the paraffin wax. These colours are highly concentrated and you need use only a tiny amount. Powders and colours that are supplied in tubes can be added direct to the paraffin wax/stearin mixture.

Because the colours can be mixed with each other and used in different strengths, you can obtain an enormous range of colours. Remember that the colour tends to fade as the wax hardens, so if you want a special shade, do a test run the day before – you can always remelt the wax if the colour is correct.

Scents

Paraffin wax is, as we have noted, odourless. However, special wax perfumes are available, and it is possible to add vegetable extracts or essences to the molten wax. Essential oils are available in chemists, some large supermarkets and in shops that sell essences for aromatherapy. Try thyme, lavender, pine, jasmine and lily-of-the-valley. These essences are expensive, but you need only use a drop or two. Do be careful not to add too much, or the resulting smell will be overpowering and unpleasant. Experiment with different fragrances and different amounts, because some just do not work.

Wicks

Apart from wax, the other essential element in a candle is the wick.

Wick is generally sold in rods or lengths of white, braided cotton that has been impregnated with chemicals to improve its burning qualities. Remember, though, that the wick itself merely delivers the melting wax to the flame. The vapours given off as the wax melts are what actually burn – not the wick.

You will be able to buy wicks from craft shops that stock candle wax. It is usually sold on cards or bobbins, and the diameter of the finished candle will determine the size of wick you need to use. To make matters easy, the wick is labelled according to the diameter of the candle for which it is suited. It is sold in increments of 1.25cm (½in), so if you want to make a candle with a finished diameter of, for example, about 5cm (2in), use the wick that is so labelled.

It is important to use the appropriate wick for the size of candle – if you do not, the candle will not burn properly. The thickest wick is used for the candles with the greatest diameter, and you should also use this thicker wick for beeswax candles, because beeswax tends to be more viscous than paraffin wax. If necessary, twist finer lengths of wick together to create a thick wick for a really fat candle. The finest wick is used for small night lights and tall, slim candles. You may also find wick reinforced with a metal thread to make it more rigid. This is sold by the metre (yard) or in shorter lengths, some of which are already attached to a metal base (also available separately). This kind can be useful when you are making candles with angled stripes.

Before it is used, the wick has to be prepared or primed. Dip lengths of ordinary wick into molten paraffin wax and then allow it to harden. Make it in batches and straighten it with your fingers as it dries.

One or two of the candles described in this book use candlewick, which is sold in lengths of about 6m (20ft). This wick is softened in warm water and plaited and twisted together to make unusual candles. If you want to experiment with this technique you may have to search out specialist suppliers.

A wicking needle (see Stockists, page 48) is useful for inserting wicks or for anchoring the wick in place

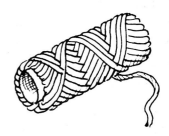

STARTING WORK

Although making candles is no messier or more dangerous than many other crafts, it is sensible to take a few precautions.

First, make sure you have sufficient time. Heating the wax and then allowing the finished candle to set and harden cannot be hurried.

You will need ample working space. You cannot pour molten wax easily into moulds if you are cramped, and you are more likely to spill wax and tip moulds over. Before you begin, cover your working surface with newspaper and lay a piece of tinfoil over this. You might also want to put newspaper on the floor to catch any drips. Have all the equipment you need close to hand — your heat source, the wax and stearin, the wicks, the dyes, a selection of moulds, wicking needles, a sugar thermometer and scales — because wax cools down quite quickly and the further you have to carry it, the more difficult your job will be.

Because wax has to be heated, you should take the obvious safety precautions. Except on very rare occasions, you will not need to heat wax directly over the heat source. More often the wax will be in a double saucepan or bain-marie. Never leave heating wax unattended, whether it is in a double saucepan or not, and do not leave saucepan handles protruding over the edge of the cooker. If the worst happens and some wax catches alight, do not try to put out the flames with water. Switch off the heat and cover the flames with a damp cloth or fire blanket or put a metal lid on the saucepan.

Preparing the Wax

Unless you are using mouldable wax, whatever kind of wax you use — powder, granules, pellets or chips — has to be melted down with stearin. Put the granules or chips in a stainless steel or aluminium double saucepan or in a metal bowl over a saucepan of boiling water and remember to keep the water in the lower saucepan topped up.

It is difficult to be precise about the temperature that is required for each kind of wax, because it varies according to the source, the type of wax you use and any additives. Because the boiling point of water is 100°C (212°F), wax heated in a double saucepan will not exceed that temperature, and most candles described here can, in fact, be made with wax heated to about 90°C (194°F). Sometimes, lower temperatures will enable you to achieve the effects you want. It is worth keeping notes about the different temperatures that give the best results.

Very occasionally, you will want a higher temperature, when the wax will have to be heated over direct heat. Take extra care whenever this is necessary.

Heating the Wax

Your kitchen cooker, whether electric or gas, will be perfectly adequate, at least for your early experiments. If you get hooked on candlemaking, you might want to think about buying a special electric pot with a thermostatic control.

Moulds

A range of moulds is essential for poured candles. There is a huge variety to choose from:

◆ Ready-made moulds: These enable you to produce the same candle over and over again. Craft shops sell them in all kinds of shapes – cylinders, stars, rectangles and squares, cones and egg-shapes – and materials, from opaque and transparent plastic to metal or rubber, which is ideal for producing candles in the shapes of fruit, flowers and so on. These commercial moulds generally make candles with wonderfully smooth surfaces.

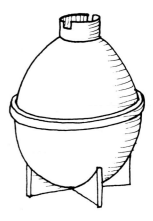

NB: Do not use stearin with rubber or other flexible moulds, as it will rot them. Use a very small amount (about ½ to 1 per cent) of Vybar (see Stockists, page 48) as a release agent instead.

◆ Home-made moulds: You will find in your home all kinds of objects that can be used as moulds. As long as it will withstand the heat of the wax and will not leak (or can be made leak-proof) and as long as it is not so shaped that you cannot remove the hardened candle, you can use almost anything that comes to hand, including bun tins, glass and rigid plastic bottles, jars and packaging of various kinds (the materials used to package pharmaceutical products and cosmetics are especially useful).

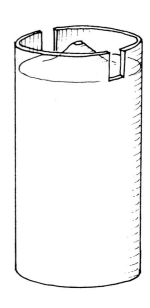

◆ Apart from containers that can be pressed into service as moulds, you may also find that sections of plastic bottles or of pipes, or terracotta plant pots (as long as they are not narrower at the top than at the base) can be used. You will need to stand such articles on modelling clay or Plasticine, making sure that the base is flat and that the sides are completely vertical. Place the modelling clay on a piece of card on your work surface and use a rolling pin or glass bottle to roll it to size and to make it flat and smooth. Then put your mould in position and add more modelling clay around the base to make absolutely certain that it is watertight. For small containers, Blu-Tack is a useful mould sealant.

◆ If you cannot find the exact shape or texture that you want, you can easily make moulds from corrugated or textured card. Draw the outline of the circle, hexagon, octagon or whatever shape you want to make on heavy card, and carefully cut out and construct the sides of the mould. Use adhesive tape to hold the sides together and make sure the bottom edge is completely surrounded with Plasticine or mould sealant.

suitable

Remember to brush the inside of all your moulds with a release agent to make it easy for you to turn out the candle when it has set. As noted above, use Vybar for rubber moulds, and mist cardboard containers with water from a plant spray or smear petroleum jelly around the inside.

Other Essentials

You will also need to make sure that the following tools and pieces of equipment are to hand before you begin:

unsuitable

◆ a wooden spoon or stick to mix the wax and dyes thoroughly

◆ a large metal pouring spoon or ladle or a jug so that you can pour the wax into the centre of the mould

◆ scissors to cut wick to length

◆ a knife to smooth the base of candles, grate wax dye and incise patterns on finished candles

◆ wicking needles for inserting wicks

◆ scales to weigh the paraffin wax and stearin

◆ sugar thermometer (available from kitchenware shops) for checking the temperature of the wax as it is heated

◆ washing-up bowl

◆ measuring jug to enable you to assess the volume of your moulds

◆ cloths and paper to wipe up spills

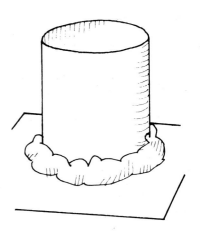

Fluted candle (see page 13); **blue heaven** (see page 45); **poured pink candle** (see page 11); **candle with golden highlights** (see page 12); **marbled candle** (see page 46).

SINGLE COLOUR CANDLES

Candles that are a single colour are very simple to make, for the moulding can be done in one stage. The instructions in this section explain the main ways in which the wick is inserted in the candle. Even if you do not want to make any of these candles, you should, at least, make yourself familiar with the wick techniques.

POURED PINK CANDLE

(Illustrated on page 10)

You will need:

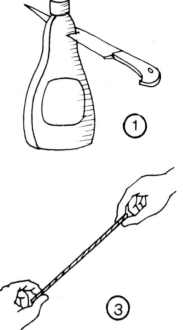

- a plastic bottle for a mould (we used a shampoo bottle)
- paraffin wax and stearin mix
- powdered wax dye
- wick (at least 1cm/½in longer than the depth of the mould)

Cut off the top of the bottle (1) and make sure it is perfectly clean. Place the paraffin wax and stearin in a double saucepan. Add a little of the wax dye (2).

Soak the wick in warm wax, pull it taut between your fingers and hold it until the wax has set (3).

Heat the wax until it reaches a temperature of 80°C (176°F) – at this point, a spot of wax dropped onto greaseproof paper sets immediately. Pour the wax into the mould.

When the surface of the wax has begun to harden but is still pliable to the touch, insert the stiff wick through the centre. It should stand upright of its own accord (see illustration 4 on page 12). You can only use this method of inserting a wick in single-colour candles.

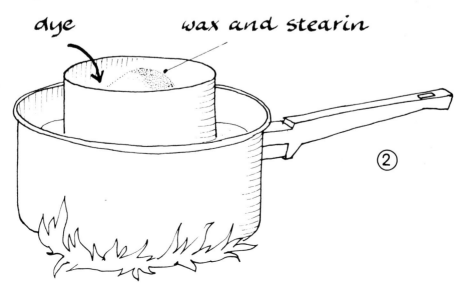

dye   wax and stearin

Leave the candle to set. You can speed up the process by standing the mould in a bowl of cold water or even by placing it in your fridge. Remove the mould. Cut it off with a craft knife, taking care not to mark the surface of the candle.

FLOATING CANDLES

(Illustrated on page 15)

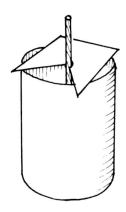

These are ideal for a party, and can be simply made by pouring the wax into pastry cutters (5).

Place each pastry cutter on tinfoil. Carefully pour in the wax, and as soon as it begins to set, insert a prepared wick.

CANDLE WITH GOLDEN HIGHLIGHTS

(Illustrated on page 10)

You will need:

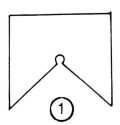

◆ a square mould made from corrugated cardboard
◆ adhesive tape
◆ scissors and craft knife
◆ wick (at least 1cm/¹/₂in longer than the mould)
◆ cardboard
◆ paraffin wax and stearin mix
◆ powdered wax dye (use a dark colour)
◆ gold paint

The mould for this candle was originally the inside packaging around a bottle of perfume. Use adhesive tape to secure all possible gaps.

Place the wax and the dye in the bain-marie and begin to melt it. Meanwhile, prepare the wick. Cut a piece of card or strong paper into the shape shown right (1). The wick can be held in the little groove in the card, which rests across the top of the mould, holding the wick upright and in the correct position (2). This method can be used for all poured candles of a fairly large diameter.

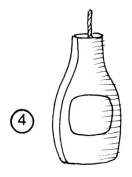

Heat the wax to the correct temperature. If it is allowed to get too hot, the wax will draw away from the wick. You can overcome this problem by adding a little more molten wax as the surface begins to harden. If the wax is not hot enough or if it was poured too quickly, bubbles may form. Make sure you tap the mould gently when you have poured in the wax.

When the wax is quite hard, remove the mould, using the craft knife to cut through the adhesive tape.

Put a minute amount of gold paint on the tip of your index finger and use the paint to add highlights to the candle. Do not try to cover the whole candle with gold – you are aiming to add subtle touches to the textured surface.

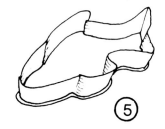

FLUTED CANDLE

(Illustrated on page 10)

You will need:

- a mould (we used large corrugated cardboard)
- adhesive tape
- Plasticine or modelling clay
- rolling pin
- board or heavyweight card
- paraffin wax and stearin mix
- powdered wax dye (we used dark blue)
- prepared wick (use the largest size)

This striking candle is easy to make. The complicated bit is to make a mould from lightweight cardboard. You may have to lift the corrugated section away from the backing card to make it flexible enough to form into a mould (1). Fasten the ends together with adhesive tape (2).

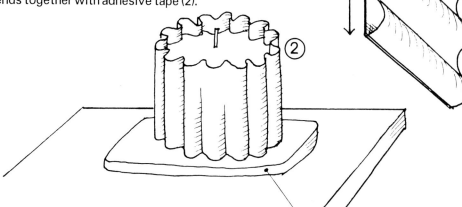

Place the Plasticine or clay on the board and use a rolling pin to flatten and shape it to form a base for the mould (3).

carefully remove Plasticine ③

Pour a small amount of molten wax into the bottom of the mould to test that it is watertight. If necessary, fill any gaps with more Plasticine. Pour in the rest of the wax in one go.

Insert the prepared wick in the candle as soon as it begins to harden. When the wax is completely set, remove the tape and then carefully lift the mould and candle away from the Plasticine.

EGG CANDLE

(Illustrated on page 15)

You will need:

- an egg-shaped mould or a blown egg
- paraffin wax and stearin mix
- wax dye (a pale, pastel shade)
- prepared wick (use the finest wick)
- wicking needle
- small piece of mould sealant or modelling clay

You can buy egg-shaped moulds, which come in two sections, with a hole in the appropriate place for the wick and a hole in the top for pouring in the wax (1). The wick is held in place in a groove in the top.

Cut a length of wick that is 3–4cm (1¼–1½in) greater than the depth of the mould. Thread it through the hole in the base of the mould and hold it firmly in place with mould sealant or modelling clay. Close the mould and tie the other end of the wick tightly around a wicking needle (2).

Carefully pour the coloured, molten wax through the hole at the top of the mould. You will find it easier if you decant the wax from the saucepan into a jug.

When the wax is completely hard, use a knife to scrape any overspill from around the joint. Remove the needle and separate the two halves of the mould. Trim the wick and, if necessary, flatten the base of the candle with the blade of a knife, warmed in hot water.

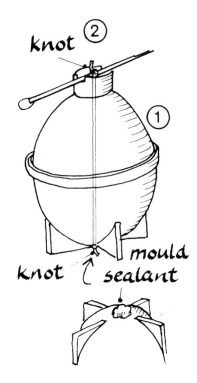

POT OF JAM

(Illustrated on page 15)

This unusual effect is entirely achieved through the choice of mould and the way in which the candle is presented and decorated.

You will need:

◆ a glass jam jar (little French pots are pretty)
◆ paraffin wax and stearin mix
◆ wax dye (choose an appetising colour)
◆ prepared wick
◆ Cellophane or small piece of gingham fabric
◆ old-fashioned label

Mix the wax so that the colour resembles a mouth-watering jam. Carefully pour the molten wax into the mould and, just as it begins to harden, insert the wick.

Write the name of the jam on the label and stick it on the front of the jar. Cover the top with Cellophane or fabric.

If you wish, add a drop of perfumed essence to the wax so that, when lit, the candle smells as well as looks delicious.

CANDLE IN A GLASS

(Illustrated on page 15)

One of the easiest ways to make candles is simply to pour the wax into an unusually shaped glass. We chose one that could be used for desserts and coloured the wax so that it looked like chocolate mousse.

If you have a tall, straight-sided glass, colour the wax to imitate a refreshing soft drink. Pour clear paraffin wax into ice cube trays and when the wax in the glass begins to set, insert the stiffened wick, a straw and 'ice cubes'.

Floating candles (see page 12)**; eggs** (see page 13)**; pot of jam** (see page 14)**; candle in a glass** (see page 14)**; blue candle with 'foam'** (see pages 41 and 46).

STRIPED CANDLES

When you are making multi-coloured candles, you will need lots of separate containers to hold the different coloured waxes and plenty of cloths or kitchen towel to wipe the containers so that you can use them again straightaway.

Wicks in these candles must be held in place with a piece of card (see page 12) or a wicking needle (see page 14).

HORIZONTAL STRIPES

YELLOW AND ORANGE CANDLE

(Illustrated on page 17)

You will need:

- ◆ a mould (we used a plastic container about 12cm/5in tall)
- ◆ paraffin wax and stearin mix
- ◆ wax dyes, ranging from yellow to orange
- ◆ prepared wick
- ◆ card or a wicking needle

Apply a release agent to the inside of the mould. Melt the wax and add yellow dye. Pour a layer into the mould and, when it begins to set, insert the wick, holding it in place at the top of the mould with card or a needle.

If you have some yellow wax left in the bain-marie, add more dye to intensify the colour. Remember, you can make the colour of the wax darker, but you cannot make it lighter. Therefore, the first layer is a pale yellow, the next layer slightly darker and so on, as you work through the spectrum from yellow to orange to red. Continue to add layers of wax until you reach the top of the container.

When you are adding layers of wax in this way, you must take especial care that the temperature of the new wax is not too high. If it is, the new layer will not bond with the one below. One way of overcoming this is to make little holes with the end of a pencil in the surface of the lower layer (1) before you add the next. This will give much more stability to the finished candle and ensure that all the layers are held firmly together (2).

When the layers of wax reach the top of the container, leave the candle to harden completely before unmoulding.

You can make several candles at the same time by this method, varying colours in different moulds.

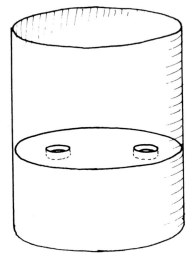

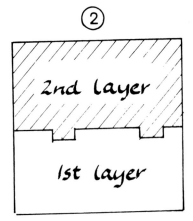

Yellow and orange candle (see page 16); **green striped candle** (see page 18); **pink and purple candle** (see page 18); **blue 'rock' candle** (see page 28); **blue striped candle** (see page 18).

It is worth making a note as you work of the different colours that you have added, in case you want to re-create a particular effect on another occasion.

To avoid cleaning the saucepan after each layer of colour is added, you should keep to a single range of colours for each candle — shades of pink or of blue or green, for example — and you should always work from lighter to darker shades. If you do want to change colours completely, you should wipe out the saucepan very carefully, while it is still warm, with an old rag or with kitchen towels.

Retouching

◆ The finished appearance of a horizontally striped candle is sometimes spoiled by splodges of wax adhering to layers of a different colour. This happens when the mould is fairly small, especially if you do not pour the new wax precisely into the centre of the mould. This happened with the blue candle illustrated on page 17. You can overcome this by going over the surface of the finished candle with a knife, shaving off vertical slivers of wax to create a many-sided candle. You can see with this candle that, because each shade was allowed to cool slightly before it was added, air bubbles formed in the wax, and these became visible when the surface was shaved slightly, adding to the individuality of the candle.

◆ The layers of the green-striped candle (see page 17) did not bond well together when it was taken from the mould. You can solve this problem by passing a heated knife blade over the loose joints. On this candle, all the joints were treated in this way, and then we went over the entire surface of the candle with a hammer, creating a series of little indentations that not only help to disguise the smoothing between layers but add an interesting texture.

◆ The pink and purple candle (see page 17) was also trimmed with a knife, but to a lesser extent than the blue-striped candle. We also applied flakes of dark red wax to the surface to enhance its appearance still further.

SLANTING STRIPES
ROUND CANDLE WITH DIAGONAL STRIPES

(Illustrated on page 20)

You will need:

◆ a cylindrical mould (we used one 11cm/4¼in across)
◆ adhesive tape, mould sealant or modelling clay
◆ a container to support the mould at an angle
◆ paraffin wax and stearin mix
◆ wax dye (we used red, orange, yellow, green and blue)
◆ primed wick
◆ wicking needle

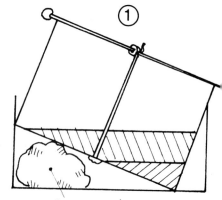

support

If you are not using a purpose-made mould, pierce a hole in the centre of the bottom. Thread the wick through the hole and hold it in place with sealant, clay or tape. Tie the wick around a needle to support it vertically in the mould.

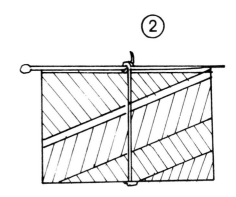

Place the mould in a large container and support one side so that it is at the angle you wish (1). Add the first layer of coloured wax. Continue to add layers of different colours until the wax is level with the edge of the mould. Wait until this layer is fairly hard before you remove the mould from the container, then pour the final layer so that the top of the candle is perfectly flat (2).

Wait until the wax is completely set before trimming the wick at the base and top. Remove the candle from the mould, and smooth the sides and top with a warm knife.

ZIG-ZAG CANDLE

(Illustrated on page 20)

This candle is a simple variant on the previous one, but the layers have been made to slant in various directions. You will find it is easier to achieve good results if you use a square or rectangular mould. Follow the instructions for the previous candle, but use strongly contrasting colours (we used two shades of green, a pink and a blue).

Add the colours as before, but turn the mould through 90 degrees each time, ending with a horizontal layer. Finish the candle as above.

TRICOLOURED DOUBLE-WICK CANDLE

(Illustrated on page 20)

You will need:

- ◆ a mould (we used a detergent carton cut to size)
- ◆ paraffin wax and stearin mix
- ◆ wax dye (we used red and two shades of blue)
- ◆ 2 prepared wicks (use the largest size)
- ◆ a container to support the mould at an angle

Apply a release agent to the mould. Prop it at an angle in the container and add the first layer of wax. When the wax has begun to set, insert the first wick, making sure that it is parallel to the sides of the mould.

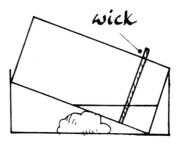

wick

When the wax is sufficiently set to hold its shape, reposition the mould in the opposite direction and add the second layer of wax. When it begins to set, insert the second wick, again making sure that it is correctly placed.

Finish off the candle on the flat by adding two more layers. Make sure that the wicks do not move. When the wax is set, remove it from the mould and neaten the edges with a warm knife.

Round candle with diagonal stripes (see page 18); zig-zag candle (see page 19); tricoloured double-wick candle (see page 19); bull's eye candle (see page 21).

CONCENTRIC CIRCLES

BULL'S EYE CANDLE

(Illustrated on page 20)

You will need:

- moulds (see below)
- paraffin wax and stearin mix
- wax dye (we used blue, pink and green)
- aluminium foil
- Plasticine or modelling clay
- prepared wick
- wicking needle
- a knife

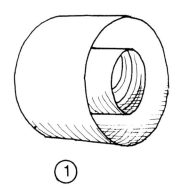

Some large plastic containers or glass jars have double stoppers which can be used to create the bull's eye effect (1). Otherwise you will have to use circular moulds that will fit inside each other (make them from card if necessary), placing them on Plasticine or modelling clay to prevent the wax from leaking out around the base. You will also need a square mould that is large enough to accommodate the diameter of the finished bull's eye.

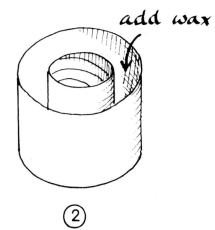

add wax

Pour the first colour into the outer of the two concentric circles (2). (In the candle illustrated this was the dark green wax.) Leave it to harden then remove it from the mould. You should have a circle of wax. Place a piece of aluminium foil on your work surface, put the circle of wax on this and surround it with Plasticine or modelling clay. Fill the centre of the circle with the second colour (we used pink), making sure that the wax is not too hot when you pour it (3).

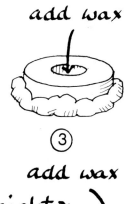

add wax

When the wax is completely set, remove the Plasticine and place the pink and green circle in the centre of a larger circular mould. Put a small weight on the pink and green circle so that it cannot move when you pour in the wax (4). This new circle of wax (pink in the candle illustrated) must be level with the top of the existing green circle. Make sure that the wax is not too hot when you pour it into the mould. If it is, the new wax will shrink from the green as it hardens. Continue to add circles in this way until you have achieved the diameter you wish.

add wax

weight

You can, of course, use the circles of wax as a candle in their own right (the wick should have been inserted before the inner circle had set hard). However, to make the candle illustrated, when the circles of wax are completely set, place them, upright, in a square mould and carefully add wax to fill. When it has set, remove from the mould and use a warm knife to smooth.

The wick can be inserted at this stage. Heat a wicking needle and make a hole right through the centre of the candle (see illustration 5 on page 22). Make sure you go right through to the other side. Insert the stiffened wick.

What Went Wrong?

◆ **Wax seeps through the base of the mould or around the hole for the wick:** Take care to seal all potential gaps with lots of Plasticine or mould sealant and add the wax very carefully, making sure that it is not too hot.

◆ **It is difficult to remove a candle from its mould:** First, check that there isn't a small rim inside the mould, preventing the candle from being turned out. Another possible reason is that the wax has not yet cooled and shrunk sufficiently. This could be because there is not enough stearin (which encourages shrinkage) in your mix. If you cannot cut or otherwise remove the mould, scrape out the wax, remelt it with a little more stearin and try again.

◆ **When you make striped candles, the different layers are not always clearly differentiated:** This happens when you add a new layer before the previous layer has hardened sufficiently or when the new wax is too hot and the previous layer has only just begun to set. There is really only one solution to this problem: hide the joins between layers with a decoration of some kind (see page 41). The alternative is to melt down the entire candle, which will probably result in a fairly unattractive, drab colour. To reuse this wax, you will have to add a strong, dark dye.

◆ **Splodges of coloured wax appear in the wrong places on the surface of a striped candle:** You have probably used a narrow mould. It is difficult to pour the wax into the centre of tall, thin moulds and almost inevitably some adheres to the sides. You can either try to remove these spots of colour with a knife or 'shave' the whole of the candle by removing slivers evenly from all over the surface.

◆ **Layers of wax seep between the edge of the mould and the candle:** This happens when the first layer has been allowed to set completely and shrink away from the edge of the mould before the next layer is added. The new, molten wax inevitably finds its way into the gap around the lower layer. When you have removed the candle from the mould, use a warm knife to remove the excess wax, then, to improve the overall appearance of the candle, dip it into a bath of clear, molten wax (see page 36).

◆ **Bubbles of air appear in the top of a candle:** The wax was probably too cold. Smooth the surface of the candle with a warm knife and improve the appearance of the candle by dipping it in clear wax (see page 36). When you have added wax to a mould, sharply tapping the side of the mould can help to prevent air bubbles forming.

◆ **The different layers of a striped candle will not bond together:** You have probably allowed each layer to set too hard before adding the next layer, or the second layer was too cold when you poured it into the mould. If you cannot get them to stick together by the use of a warm knife, you will have to dismantle the candle and begin again.

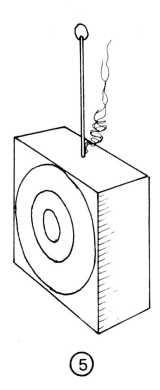

⑤

ADVANCED TECHNIQUES

As we have seen, wax can be used to make a wide variety of shapes. However, you don't always need to use a mould to create an interesting candle. In this section we look at some of the ways you can roll, shape, cut, twist and otherwise use wax to make some interesting and attractive candles. These techniques can be combined to make even more original models.

ROLLED CANDLES

Basic Technique

You will need:

- a sheet of wax (either smooth or honeycomb-patterned)
- wick (at least 1cm/½in longer than the depth of the sheet of wax)

This technique is ideal for sheets of beeswax. If you are working in a warm room, the wax should be sufficiently pliable to roll. If it is especially cold, try warming it very gently with a hair-dryer. When the wax is malleable, place the wick about 3cm/1in from one of the short edges of the sheet (1). Turn over this edge and press it down firmly against the wick. Roll the wax away from you, keeping the roll as tight as you can and making sure that the edges are level (2).

To make a cone, cut a sheet of wax in half diagonally with a craft knife, then proceed as before (3).

Seal the end of the roll by pressing it with the blade of a knife (see illustration 4, page 24). Trim and smooth the base with a warm blade.

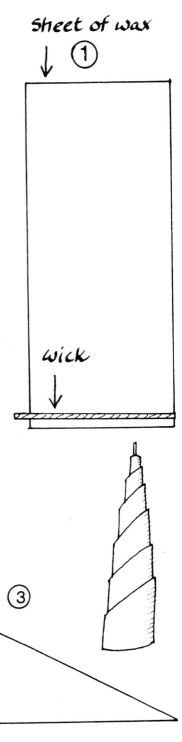

Sheet of wax ① wick

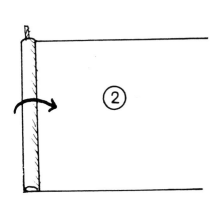

②

③

PLEATED WHITE CANDLE

(Illustrated on page 25)

You will need:

- ◆ a sheet of wax measuring about 40 x 20cm (16 x 8in)
- ◆ wick about 11cm (4½in) long
- ◆ craft knife

Cut the sheet of wax in half so that you have two pieces each measuring about 40 x 10cm (16 x 4in). Roll one of these rectangles around the wick to make a simple rolled candle.

Take the other rectangle and pleat it to form a series of neat concertina folds (1). Then arrange the folded wax around the rolled candle, opening out the pleats evenly around the edge.

Use a pointed knife to press the wax to the inner core (2), and heat the blade to ensure that the wax adheres firmly where it touches the centre.

MULTI-COLOURED ROLLED CANDLE

(Illustrated on page 25)

You will need:

- ◆ a sheet of translucent wax measuring about 40 x 20cm (16 x 8in)
- ◆ sheet of white paper
- ◆ wax crayons
- ◆ wick about 23cm (9in) long

Place the smooth side of the wax sheet on the white paper. Use the crayons to apply colour to about one-third of the wax. Do not be too precise; make several fairly large splashes of colour (see the sketch below). Remember that the colours you apply will be seen through the translucent wax. Several layers of colour will give a completely different effect seen from the other side. Lift the sheet from time to time to check the effect.

When you are satisfied, position the wick on the short end furthest away from the coloured area and roll up the candle tightly, finishing it off neatly as before.

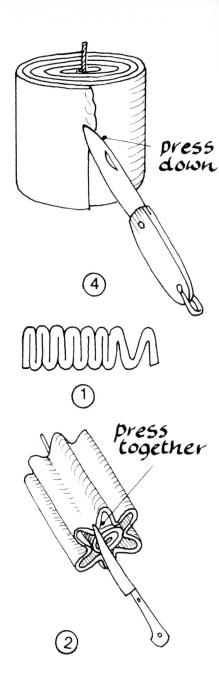

press down

④

①

press together

②

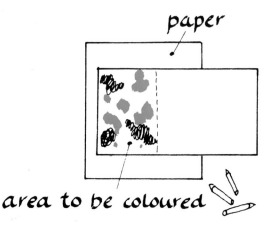

paper

area to be coloured

Countryside candle (see page 26); white rolled candles decorated with a bird and with a cockerel; multi-coloured rolled candle (see page 24); pleated white candle (see page 24).

COUNTRYSIDE CANDLE

(Illustrated on page 25)

You will need:

- ◆ 3 sheets of translucent wax, each 40 x10cm (16 x 4in)
- ◆ wick about 12cm (5in) long
- ◆ craft knife
- ◆ sheet of white paper
- ◆ wax crayons

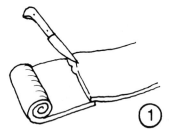

Place the wick against the short end of one of the sheets of wax, matt side up, and roll the wax tightly around it. Join the other two rectangles on as you continue to roll the candle around the wick, using a knife to smooth the joins (1).

When you get to the end, mark the position of the end on the underlying piece of wax (2) and unroll this section. Place this piece of wax on the paper and draw around its outline (3). Remove the wax and draw on the paper the scene you will transfer to the candle (4).

Place the drawing under the sheet of wax, aligning the edge of the drawing with the edge of the wax. Use wax crayons to colour the scene which will be visible through the wax. When you are satisfied with the design, re-roll the candle, smoothing the end into place with a warm knife as before.

final turn

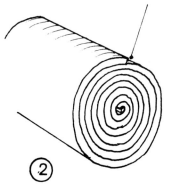

trace the outline

paper

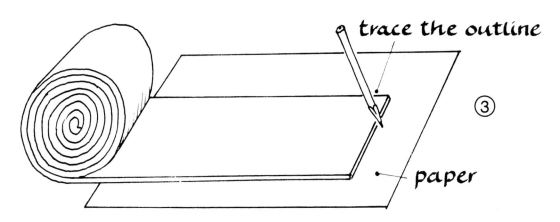

HAND-MOULDED CANDLES

Basic Technique

For the candles in this section you will need some squares of proprietary mouldable wax.

Break the squares of wax into smallish pieces. Make sure your hands are warm before you begin to work the wax.

You can blend two colours to make new shades. If you stop kneading just before they are completely mixed, the wax will look like marble. You can gild it by dusting your hands with a small amount of gold powder before you begin kneading.

The wick is inserted when you have finished work on the candle. Special wicks with a metal core are useful for this work. Make a hole in the finished piece with a heated wicking needle. The hole needs to be just slightly larger than the wick. Insert the wick, and add a tiny piece of wax to cover the hole at the base. When the candle is lit, the warmth of the flame will cause the wax to melt slightly and fill the hole around the wick. If you do not have any of the special metal core wicks, use a prepared wick (see page 11).

You can coat your finished candles by dipping them in a bath of clear, warm paraffin wax.

You can combine modelling wax with other techniques. The flowers and leaves of the African violet candle illustrated on page 39 were made in this way. Press and smooth the pieces of wax until they are as thin as possible, use scissors to cut them to shape and carefully add curves and folds to make them look natural.

GREEN AND RED SNAKE

(Illustrated on page 40)

You will need:

- 9 squares of each colour (we used red and green)
- a bowl of water no warmer than 40°C (104°F)
- wick
- wicking needle

Keeping the two colours separate, knead the squares until you can make two long, smooth 'snakes'. Immerse them in the lukewarm water, and then twine together, using the illustration as a guide or letting your imagination have free rein. If one of the strips of wax breaks, you will have to dry the ends before they can be rejoined.

Remove the finished piece from the water and allow it to drain. Smooth the surface with your fingers, and use a knife or spatula to add the details. Place the candle on your working surface and make sure that it will stand upright without wobbling. Make a hole through the centre with a hot wicking needle and insert the wick.

CANDLES MODELLED FROM 'WHIPPED' WAX

It is just as easy to model wax that you have made in a saucepan in the normal way. Take great care that it is not too hot to handle. You will find that a suitable consistency – neither too hard, nor too soft – occurs when the wax has started to cool down and has just begun to set. To achieve this consistency, beat the hot wax with a fork (make sure it is in a high-sided container before you do this).

BLUE 'ROCK' CANDLE

(Illustrated on page 17)

You will need:

- 2 colours of whipped wax
- prepared wick
- wicking needle
- blowtorch (optional)

Take small pieces of wax and mould them with your fingers, pressing them together and mixing up the colours. Press the pieces together between your hands to make sure that the candle will not fall apart.

When you are satisfied with your design, use a hot wicking needle to make a hole through the centre and insert the wick.

If you wish (and as we did), use a blowtorch so that the surface of the wax melts slightly and runs together a little. The heat from the flame will cause the wax to melt sufficiently to make the colours run together and create new shades.

ICE-CREAM SUNDAE

(Illustrated on page 29)

You will need:

- a small sundae dish (glass or metal)
- an ice-cream scoop (optional)
- whipped wax (various colours)
- prepared wick (use the largest size)
- wicking needle

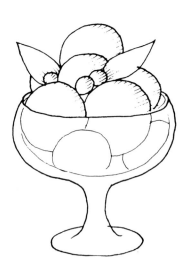

Using the scoop or moulding by hand, form the wax into balls. Arrange them in the sundae dish, previously warmed with hot water and carefully dried.

If the 'scoops' do not bond well, run a warm knife between them to soften the wax until the balls hold together. Alternatively, slip one or two small bits of molten wax between them to keep them together.

Make a hole in the candle with a hot wicking needle and insert the stiffened wick, or slip it between the 'scoops', filling the space with warm wax.

Ice-cream sundae (see page 28); **fruit tarts** (see page 38).

Red and green sand candles (see page 31); blue and green soldered candle (see page 32); navy blue square candle (see page 45).

SAND CANDLES

(Illustrated on page 30)

This technique enables you to make candles of all kinds of shapes and sizes without a mould.

They need very hot wax, at least 93°C (200°F), and it is impossible to achieve this heat in a double saucepan. You must put the wax in a thick-bottomed saucepan and heat it very, very carefully. Use your sugar thermometer to check the temperature at frequent intervals. Take every possible precaution. Keep a damp towel to hand in case the wax does catch fire – and whatever you do, never try to put out the fire by pouring water on it. Children should never be allowed to make candles by this method.

However, with precautions, these are very easy candles to make. When the hot wax comes into contact with the damp sand, it creates the 'crust' that is so typical of these candles. The end results vary according to the kind of sand that you use. Make sure that it is not too damp, because when too much moisture is present the wax cools down too quickly, spreading only a little way into the sand and creating a thin crust.

Basic Technique

You will need:

- a washing-up bowl or large box full of sand
- suitable objects to make impressions in the sand
- wax
- powdered wax dyes
- prepared wick
- sugar thermometer registering temperatures up to at least 150°C (300°F)

Dampen the sand in the bowl and tamp the surface slightly so that it is perfectly flat but not too compressed.

Take the object chosen to make the impression in the sand. You could use the bottom of a bottle or a heavy ashtray, for example. Press it firmly into the sand and then remove it carefully. If necessary, smooth and strengthen the impression, or use your fingers, a piece of wood or a cylinder to elaborate it (see illustration 1 on page 32).

Heat and colour the wax (see above), making sure that you have plenty – some of it will seep into the sand, so you will need more than for an ordinary candle of a comparable size. Carefully pour the molten wax into the prepared impression. As soon as the wax begins to set, insert the wick.

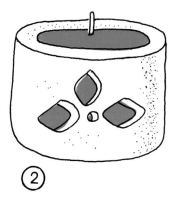

When the candle is completely set, remove it from the sand. Shake and brush away the loose sand. You can then leave it as it is, simply neatening the top with a sharp knife. Or, if the crust is thick, you could carve a pattern in the sides with a sharp pointed knife (see illustration 2).

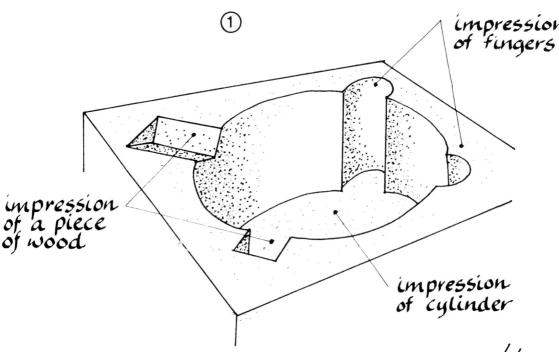

① impression of fingers

impression of a piece of wood

impression of cylinder

'SOLDERED' CANDLES

(See illustration on page 30)

You will need:

- moulds (you need long, thin boxes)
- wax (we used blue and green)
- a long prepared wick
- blowtorch (a small gas-powered one is ideal)
- tinfoil

Make two green and two blue rectangles in the moulds. Remove them when they are set.

Cover your work surface with an ovenproof or fireproof mat covered with tinfoil. Place two of the wax rectangles side by side on the foil and lay a stiffened wick along the join between them. Pass the flame of the blowtorch quickly along the length of the wick and the junction between the two rectangles (1).

Place the other blocks above and below the central joint of the first blocks (2). Use the blowtorch to slightly soften the joints at the sides of the top and bottom rectangles to hold them in position. If necessary, neaten and flatten the bottom of the candle with a warm knife.

Use the knife to incise a small cross where the wick protrudes. You will need a fairly wide holder to catch the quantity of drips this candle produces when lit.

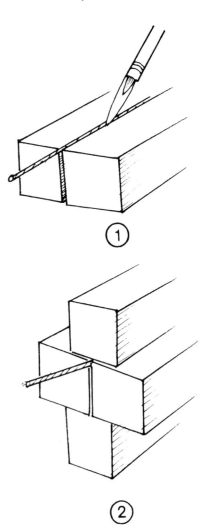

WOVEN CANDLES
BALL OF STRING CANDLE

(Illustrated on page 40)

You will need:

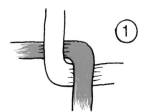

♦ 2m (about 6ft) of candlewick
♦ bowl of lukewarm water (no warmer than 40°C/104°F)

Soak the candlewick in water to make it malleable. Quickly roll it into a ball and pull out one end. When it is dry, this makes an unusual and decorative candle. When it is lit, it will burn rather erratically, so it needs to be handled carefully.

YELLOW 'MACRAMÉ' CANDLE

(Illustrated on page 40)

You will need:

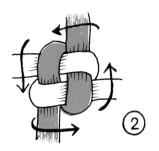

♦ 2 lengths of candlewick, each about 1m (3ft)
♦ bowl of lukewarm water

Soak the lengths of candlewick in water and work carefully, following illustrations 1 and 2 on this page to make a neatly plaited candle. When finished, straighten it if necessary and hold under cold running water until the wax has set.

Trim back three of the free ends, leaving one standing upright (3). Flatten and smooth the base with a warm knife.

DIPPED CANDLES

(Illustrated on page 43)

This is the way in which candles were traditionally made, and it fell from favour only because it requires a great deal of patience. These candles have become popular again in recent years, and even if you decide not to make them yourself, the method can be adapted and used to create interesting effects on poured or moulded candles.

It is more economical to make two candles at a time by this method.

You will need:

♦ a piece of H-shaped card (see illustration 1 on page 34)
♦ wick that is twice as long as the finished length of the candle, plus 10–12cm (4–5in)
♦ a straight-sided container that is deep enough to hold the hot wax, or a special dipping pot (see Stockists, page 48)
♦ coloured wax

Soak both ends of the wick in wax up to the desired height of the finished candle. Allow the wax to harden. Hang the wick over the piece of card (see illustration 2 on page 34) and plunge into the warm wax again. Allow to drain, leave to dry and harden for a minute. Repeat as often as necessary.

You need to arrange somewhere where you can suspend the wicks to drain and harden between dippings. You will find it far too tiring to try and hold them all the time.

Try to dip to the same level throughout the process, and to keep the wax at a constant temperature. If it gets too cool, the dipping will not be even. To make a tapering candle like the one on page 43, reduce the depth to which you dip each time, so that the base is much thicker than the top part.

When you have achieved the shape you want but while the wax is still soft, use your fingers to create more unusual and individual effects. For example, try pressing the wax to create smooth undulations down the sides. Alternatively, roll it between two sheets of damp glass to make it perfectly smooth. Or simply leave it as it is.

Smooth and flatten the base with a warm knife so that the candle sits squarely. Trim the wicks to length.

If you plan to make a lot of candles by the dipping method, take a length of wood and hammer in a series of nails about 10cm (4in) apart along one side (3). Suspend the wick over two nails if you are making two candles or fasten a single wick to a nail if you want to make just one candle.

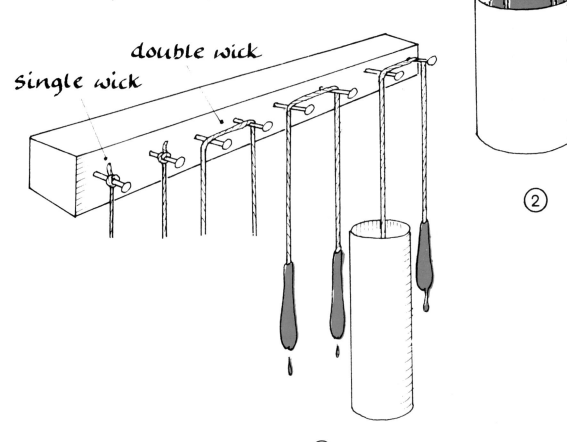

double wick

single wick

① ② ③

FANTASY CANDLES

When you have mastered all the techniques described in the previous sections, you can combine them to make all kinds of unusual and interesting candles. Here are just a few of the ways in which you can experiment for yourself.

WHITE CANDLE WITH COLOURED STRIPES

(Illustrated on page 37)

You will need:

- a cylindrical mould (preferably transparent if possible), coated with a release agent
- mouldable wax (you will need a variety of colours)
- paraffin wax and stearin mix
- prepared wick

Work the mouldable wax in your hands to make long strips. Press these against the sides of the mould. Add the molten wax. Before it sets but just as the surface begins to harden, insert the wick.

PINK AND GREEN CANDLE

(Illustrated on page 37)

You will need:

- ice cube tray
- a cylindrical mould
- paraffin wax and stearin mix
- wax dye (pink and shades of green)
- prepared wick

Make several shades of coloured green wax and pour into the ice cube tray. When they have set, turn them out of the moulds and pile them, higgledy-piggledy, into the cylindrical mould. Insert the wick, making sure that it is completely vertical. Add pale pink wax to the mould, keeping the wick in place with card or on a wicking needle.

BLUE CANDLE

(Illustrated on page 37)

You will need:

- discs of stearin
- wax dye (use a powder if possible)
- a wide-mouthed container with an airtight seal
- uncoloured wax
- prepared wick
- a mould

Put the discs and a little dye in the container. Seal it and shake energetically. The discs should become coloured. Put them in the mould, pressing down well. Insert the wick. Fill the mould with molten uncoloured wax.

PINK AND WHITE CANDLE

(Illustrated on page 37)

You will need:

- discs of paraffin wax
- a casserole or large dish
- a spoon
- a mould that can withstand high temperature
- wax (pink)
- prepared wick
- wicking needle
- a hammer

Put the discs of wax in a casserole and place it over direct heat, watching it carefully until they begin to melt (see page 8). As soon as the discs look as if they are beginning to melt, scoop them out with a spoon and place them in the mould, pressing them down. Leave to set, then remove.

Pour 1–2cm (about ½in) of very hot pink wax into the mould. Replace the half-melted wax discs, then slowly fill the mould with pink wax right to the top. The discs will melt a little more as the new wax is added.

When the wax has hardened, use a hot wicking needle to make a hole through the centre and insert the wick. Use the hammer to make a pattern of indentations.

CANDLE WITH WHITE MARBLING

(Illustrated on page 37)

You will need:

- powdered wax
- wax of different colours
- a mould, preferably transparent
- prepared wick
- wicking needle

Pour a layer of fairly hot coloured wax into the mould. Before it has cooled down, swirl the mould around so that the wax adheres to the sides in an irregular pattern. Next add a thick layer of the powdered wax to the mould and press it down firmly.

Add a fresh layer of very hot molten wax to the desired height of the finished candle. When the wax has hardened, remove the candle from the mould and make a hole for the wick with a heated wicking needle.

The white area (created by the powdered wax) tends to crumble. Overcome this by smoothing with a warm knife.

Pink and green candle (see page 35); green candle with surface
decoration; pink and white candle (see page 36); candle with white
marbling (see page 36); white candle with coloured stripes (see page
35); blue candle (see page 35); deep pink and white candle.

TWO-STAGE CANDLE

(Illustrated on page 43)

This is a simple poured candle, made from red wax. It is surrounded by a layer of pleated sheet wax (see page 24). The pleats have been highlighted with red nail varnish.

FRUIT TARTS

(Illustrated on page 29)

You will need:

◆ pastry cases
◆ wax (coloured to resemble pastry)
◆ mouldable wax (in various colours)
◆ short lengths of prepared wick
◆ wicking needle

The pastry case moulds become part of the candle. Pour in some hot, pastry-coloured wax and swirl around to coat the sides. Repeat until the base and sides are thickly and evenly coated. Use the mouldable wax to shape fruits, colouring them as appropriate. Press the 'fruit' into the bottom of each 'pastry case'. If necessary, use a little wax glue (a soft, sticky wax) to hold them together. Heat the wicking needle and make a hole in the centre of each tart. Insert the wick.

AFRICAN VIOLETS

(Illustrated on page 39)

You will need:

◆ a mould (use a plant pot for the correct shape)
◆ mould sealant
◆ wax (coloured to resemble terracotta and earth)
◆ mouldable wax (in various colours)
◆ prepared wick and metal core wick
◆ wax crayons
◆ wax glue

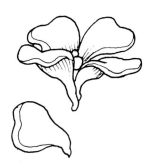

The plant pot: Fill the hole with mould sealant. Pour some molten terracotta-coloured wax into the mould and swirl it around until the wax covers the sides and base. Repeat the process until the mould is covered with a layer of wax 2–3mm (about 1in) deep. Leave to harden.

Fill the wax plant pot with earth-coloured wax. When the wax begins to harden, insert one or two prepared wicks. As soon as the wax has hardened, remove the mould.

The flowers: Model the petals and leaves from mouldable wax. Create subtle shades by lightly blending the colours. Place the leaves around the edge of the pot, pressing down firmly at their bases. If necessary, use a little wax glue. Fix the petals with a tiny piece of metal core wick.

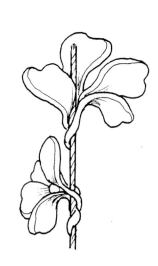

When you light this candle, light the wicks in the flowers before you light the long wicks.

African violets (see page 38); candles with applied dried flowers and
leaves (see page 44).

Green and red snake (see page 27); red, white and blue candle (see page 42); yellow macramé candle (see page 33); yellow and mauve candle (see page 41); white candle with applied wax decoration; decoupage stars (see page 41); candle with red dots (see page 41); baked bean candle (see page 42); ball of string candle (see page 33).

DECORATIVE TECHNIQUES

There are dozens of ways in which you can decorate a plain home-made or shop-bought candle, adding texture, colour and patterns. Just a few of these methods are described here, and you can build on these techniques to find your own ways of adding interest and individuality.

APPLIED WAX DECORATION

DECOUPAGE STARS

(Illustrated on page 40)

We cut stars from leftover coloured wax, pressing them carefully into the wax of the candle with the fingertips.

CANDLE WITH RED DOTS

(Illustrated on page 40)

This candle is decorated with circles cut from a sheet of wax with something like the cap of a pen. Press in place with your fingers or use tiny amounts of wax glue.

YELLOW AND MAUVE CANDLE

(Illustrated on page 40)

This candle is decorated with mouldable wax to create a relief pattern. So that the shapes adhere well, stretch them slightly as you press them in position, and smooth the edges with a warm knife.

'Foam' Wax

(Illustrated on page 15)

Whip molten wax with a fork until it is like foam. Pile it around the base of a candle or use a spatula or spoon to press it over the sides (1).

Coloured Wax

One of the simplest ways of enhancing a plain candle is to pour or drip coloured wax around it. Depending on how you hold the candle, the wax will run in differing patterns (2).

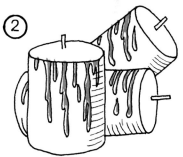

BAKED BEAN CANDLE

(Illustrated on page 40)

Dip a simple, shop-bought candle into clear, hot wax and then roll it quickly in orange wax pellets (sold for making batik fabrics). Place them in a flat tray on your work surface so as to cover the candle evenly. Use wax glue to hold any recalcitrant pellets in place.

Dipped Decorations

Dipping a plain candle in a bath of wax of a different colour is a quick and easy way to add interest. The red, white and blue candle illustrated on page 40 was created by dipping the top and bottom of a plain white candle into red wax. The applied circles of blue wax serve both as additional decoration and to disguise the join between the two colours.

You can also dip a candle into several successive baths of the same colour, each time dipping less and less of the candle so that the base is much wider than the top (3).

Keep a careful eye on the temperature of the wax. If it is too hot, the wax already on the candle will simply melt; if it is too cold, it will form lumps — although this, of course, may be an effect you want.

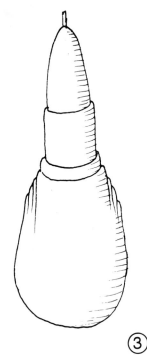

(3)

INCISED DECORATION

Hammered Patterns

An easy way to enliven a rather plain candle is to hammer the surface. You can make the pattern regular or not. We used this technique on the green-striped candle illustrated on page 17 and on the white and pink candle on page 37.

Incising Cold Wax

This kind of decoration can be done with a pointed knife, a nail, a needle or almost any other sharp implement. The cuts should not be very deep, and you can give the decorated candle a glossy coat by dipping it in a bath of clear wax or by using a paintbrush to apply a coat of wax.

Incising with Heated Tools

Any heated metal tool will leave an impression on the wax, and you can try this to add some subtle texturing to a plain candle. Heat the tool in a gas flame (use a small blowtorch if you have one), but remember to keep the flame away from the candle itself.

Textured decoration (see page 44); dipped candle (see page 33); marbled candle (see page 36); incised two-colour decoration (see page 44); engraved pattern (see page 44); two-stage candle (see page 38).

Textured Decorations

(Illustrated on page 43)

Dip a plain candle into a bath of a wax of a different colour to give it a smooth, even coat. When the wax is hard, use a heated tool to remove the top coat so that the underlying wax is visible. You can use a variety of tools for this purpose; a nail or metal knitting needle with a fairly sharp tip will serve well. Begin at the top, and incise a series of straight lines, radiating in a V-shape from the wick. The wax removed by the tool will drip down the sides, and if you wish, you can add a touch of black wax polish, applied with a soft cloth, to provide the finishing touch.

Engraved Patterns

(Illustrated on page 43)

Heated nail-heads of different sizes can be used to decorate a dipped candle. Make sure that they are not too hot, then work quickly to cover the sides of the candle with a pattern of large and small holes.

Incised Two-colour Decoration

(Illustrated on page 43)

This is an excellent way of decorating a plain white candle that has been dipped in a bath of a strongly contrasting colour. To achieve this kind of pattern, you will need a U- or V- shaped gouging tool.

Heat the tool, then use it to remove the applied layer in a pattern. We chose regularly spaced, wavy lines. You will have to work quickly and reheat the tool from time to time. If you wish, dip the decorated candle in a bath of clear paraffin wax to give it a glossy finish.

OTHER MATERIALS

Candles can be decorated with non-wax materials, which can be pressed into the wax fixed with wax glue then covered with a thin coat of clear paraffin wax. Very pretty results can be achieved by pressing dried leaves and flowers to a plain white candle — try some delicate grasses or ferns, or use dried petals to create whole flowers. You can also use silver and gold paints or glitter powder dotted on with your fingers before coating with clear wax.

RECYCLED WAX

Finally, here are a few suggestions for making candles from the wax that is left over from other projects or for reusing wax from candles that haven't turned out as well as you had hoped.

NAVY BLUE SQUARE CANDLE

(Illustrated on page 30)

This candle can be made from the wax that is left over after a candlemaking session – the bits that are left in moulds, slivers of coloured wax that have been removed from patterned candles and so on. Remelt all the bits and add a good, deep colour. We used navy blue, but any dark shade would do. It's best to use a colour that is much darker than the colour of the remelted wax. If you do not add a strong, dark shade, the resulting candle will look rather dull and drab.

We used a simple, square mould, and applied a release agent to make certain that the candle could be easily turned out. As soon as the wax began to set, the prepared wicks were inserted – we used two – and then we decorated the top of the candle with rows of coloured wax pellets.

BLUE HEAVEN

(Illustrated on page 10)

You will need:

- an old candle
- wicking needle or metal knitting needle
- prepared wick
- a mould that has a diameter larger than that of the candle by at least 3cm (1in)
- coloured wax

Heat the wick needle and make a hole in the centre of the old candle, just next to the wick. Make the hole so that you can remove the old wick; you should be able to pull it out. Replace it with the new, stiffened wick.

Place the old candle in the centre of the mould, supporting the wick on a piece of card. Carefully pour in the coloured wax so that it completely encircles the old candle. If the new wax is the same colour as the old candle, the new candle will look as if it were made in a single colour. If it is a different colour, you will have a candle with a coloured core. The new wax must be at least 1.5cm (½in) thick all round.

We used a very smooth mould and poured in the wax in such a way that little air bubbles appeared on the surface of the wax, which give an interestingly textured appearance to the candle.

bore a hole

old wick

remove old wick

insert new wick

BLUE CANDLE WITH 'FOAM'

(Illustrated on page 15)

You will need:

- a white reject candle (use one of your experiments that didn't quite come off)
- coloured wax and stearin
- a spoon
- a knife

Soften the candle and use your fingers to mould and shape it so that it is spread out and flattened all around the base. If you prefer, use a fork to whip the wax into 'foam', and use your hand or a spatula to smooth and spread it at the base.

The top part of the candle is covered with a layer of molten coloured wax and stearin. You can either use a spoon to pour the molten wax over the candle or you can dip the candle in a bath of the molten wax before you begin to decorate the base. When the wax has set hard, use a knife to cut through the coloured layer to reveal the original wax beneath (use the illustration on page 15 as a guide).

MARBLED CANDLE

(Illustrated on page 10)

You will need:

- pieces of wax in your chosen colours (we used left-over pieces in shades of pink, crimson, purple and so on)
- a mould, preferably transparent
- prepared wick
- uncoloured paraffin wax

Chop the coloured wax into pieces that are more or less all the same size. You may need to use a hammer to break very large pieces (if you do this, wrap them in a cloth beforehand). Put all the pieces straight into the mould. If you are using a transparent mould, you can try to arrange the wax chunks so that the colours are evenly distributed around the sides of the mould, but this is not essential.

Insert the wick, making sure that it is placed centrally in the mould and that it is perfectly straight. Support the top of the wick, using a piece of card or something similar to ensure that it cannot move when the wax melts.

Heat the paraffin wax to the correct temperature. This type of candle works best when the wax used for this stage is more translucent than the coloured chunks. This makes it possible to see the range of colours that you have used.

One problem with candles made in this way is that they often do not burn well. This is largely because the wax/stearin mix is not in ideal proportions to create a steady, bright flame. If you find that this happens, use these candles simply for decoration rather than for providing light.

CONTENTS

STOCKIST INFORMATION

Candle Makers Supplies, 28 Blythe Road, London W14 0HA. Tel: 0171-602 4031. Fax: 0171-602 2796. Shop and mail order service for everything you need - all types of wax, stearin, Vybar, dyes, wax glue, wicks and a range of sundries. Catalogue available.

Covent Garden Candle Company, 30 The Market, Covent Garden, London WC2E 8RE. Shop with a full range of products including introductory kit. Shop and mail order service: 50 New King's Road, London SW6 4LS. Tel: 0171-736 0740. Catalogue available.

Specialist Crafts PO Box 247, Leicester, LE1 9QS. Tel: 0116-251 0405. Fax: 0116-251 5015. Suppliers of a huge range of art and craft materials. Candlemaking products include wax kettles and dipping pots, mouldeable wax and cutters. Catalogue available for a small charge, refundable with purchase.

Trylon Ltd., Thrift Street, Woolaston, Northants. NN29 7QJ. Tel: 01933-664275. Fax: 01933-664960. Mail order only; full range of products including beeswax, moulds and mould seal, dyes, thermometers and wicking needles. Catalogue available.

FURTHER READING

Candlemaking: Creative Designs and Techniques by David Constable (Search Press). For serious candlemakers, a marvellous range of ideas and effects.

The New Candle Book by Gloria Nichol (Lorenz Books). Some techniques plus ideas for displaying, decorating and using candles.

The
CRAFTY HANDS
Collection

Creative Candles
Face Painting & Fancy Dress
Perfect Parties
Rag Dolls
Salt Dough Models
Simple Projects in Patchwork

First published in English in Great Britain
1995 by Aurum Press Ltd
25 Bedford Avenue, London WC1B 3AT

Translated by Lydia Darbyshire

English translation © Aurum Press 1995

First published as *Nouvelles Bougies*
1986 by Éditions Fleurus
11 rue Duguay-Trouin, 75006 Paris, France

A catalogue record for this book is available from the British Library

ISBN 1 85410 373 3

Printed in Italy